# What Can We Learn About Animals?

HOUGHTON MIFFLIN HARCOURT

**PHOTOGRAPHY CREDITS:** (c) ©Ellen Isaacs/Alamy Images; 3 (b) ©Ellen van Bodegom/Getty Images; 4 (tl) ©Joseph Van Os/Getty Images; 4 (bl) ©Ellen Isaacs/Alamy Images; 4 (tr) ©David Courtenay/Oxford Scientific/Getty Images; 4 (br) ©Fotolia; 5 (t) PhotoDisc/Getty Images; 5 (b) ©HMH; 6 (b) ©Pan Xunbin/Shutterstock; 7 (t) ©Christopher McGowan/Alamy Images; 8 (bl) ©Mike Hill/Alamy Images; 8 (br) ©Hoberman Collection/Terra/Corbis; 9 (tl) ©Richard Wear/Design Pics/Corbis; 9 (tr) ©Tim Pleasant/Shutterstock; 10 (bl) Stockbyte/Getty Images; 10 (br) ©Stan Fellerman/Corbis

Printed in Mexico

ISBN: 978-0-544-07226-8

4 5 6 7 8 9 10 0908 21 20 19 18 17 16 15 14

4500469985          A B C D E F G

## Be an Active Reader!

Look at these words.

| | |
|---|---|
| adaptation | larva |
| life cycle | pupa |
| reproduce | tadpole |

Look for answers to these questions.

What is an adaptation?

How do animals use their body parts to move?

How do animals use their body parts to eat?

How do adaptations allow animals to live where they do?

What is an animal's life cycle?

## What is an adaptation?

A duck has webbed feet. Ducks use webbed feet to swim. Not all animals have webbed feet. Webbed feet are an adaptation. An adaptation is a body part or behavior that helps animals survive in their environments.

**Webbed feet work well in water.**

## How do animals use their body parts to move?

Animals have different body parts. Some body parts allow animals to move. A bird uses its wings to fly. A dog uses its legs to run. An ape uses its long arms to swing through branches. Polar bears use their big feet to keep from breaking through the ice.

wings

arms

legs

feet

Many animals have legs. Animals use their legs to move. Some animals have two legs. Chickens have two legs. Some animals have lots of legs. Some centipedes have 30 or more legs! Some animals use more than one body part to move. Birds use their wings and legs.

| Body Part | Animal |
| --- | --- |
| legs and feet | birds, frogs, dogs |
| arms, legs, and feet | monkeys |
| wings | birds, moths, flies, butterflies |
| scales | snakes |
| fins and tails | fish |
| flippers and tails | dolphins |

## How do animals use their body parts to eat?

Birds use their beaks to catch and eat food. Birds can have short or long beaks. You can tell what a bird eats by the shape of its beak.

A dog uses its mouth to eat. Anteaters use their long tongues to lick up bugs. Butterflies have tubes for mouths. They suck up nectar with the tubes.

**This bird uses its beak to eat nuts and fruits.**

**This horse uses its flat teeth to eat plants.**

Adaptations allow animals to eat. Animals use their teeth to eat. Teeth come in all shapes and sizes. A horse has flat teeth for chewing plants. A lion has sharp teeth for tearing meat.

## How do adaptations allow animals to live where they do?

Camels can live without water for more than a week. They can live without food for months! Camels have long eyelashes to keep out the desert sand.

Giraffes have long necks. They can reach the tops of trees. Their long tongues rip leaves off plants.

camel

giraffe

**polar bear**

**alligator**

Polar bears have clear fur and black skin. Sunlight shines through the fur and warms their skin. Polar bears have so much fur that it looks white. Their color lets them blend into the snow and ice.

Alligators have long, heavy tails. They use the tails to knock prey into the water.

# What is an animal's life cycle?

Animals grow and change. The changes that happen during an animal's life make up its life cycle.

All animals reproduce, or have young. Chickens and many kinds of fish hatch from eggs.

Dogs and cats have young that are born live.

**Chicks hatch and puppies are born.**

Puppies look like their parents when they are born. Other animals do not look like their parents when they are born. These animals go through big changes during their life cycles. A moth is first an egg, then a larva, and then a pupa. A tadpole becomes a frog.

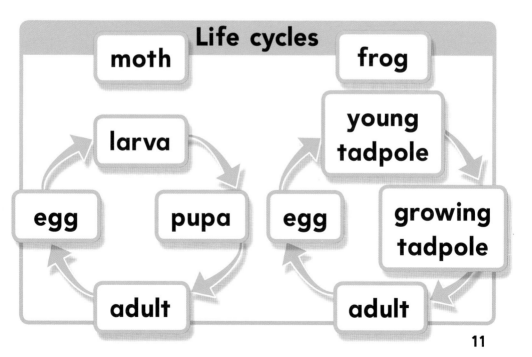

**Life cycles**

moth

larva

egg    pupa

adult

frog

young tadpole

egg    growing tadpole

adult

**Parents and Their Young**

Find pictures in magazines and classroom books of young animals and their parents. For each family, talk with a friend about how the animals look the same or different. Then choose one animal family and draw your own picture of it.

 **What Is a Zoologist?**

A zoologist is a scientist who studies animals and animal life. Write about whether you would like to be a zoologist.